E N D A N G [E](...)

Eyes on the Endangered

A Primer on Endangered Mammals

To Sophie, Caroline + Emma

Judy Mart

Judith Kruger Martin

Dedication

This book is dedicated to my incredible children, Dane and Tawni,

who constantly motivate me to go one step further.

I hope I've done the same for them.

And to my coworker, Marilyn, for your inspiration.

Table of Contents

Introduction

The Problem is Greater Than You May Think

Can you name five animals that are currently at risk of extinction?

Most people are unaware of the crisis facing our wildlife. I was clueless until I began to research information about the animals I photographed at my local zoo. I soon discovered that there are currently more than 1,500 mammal species that may not survive in the wild without assistance from the humans that share the planet with them. They are at risk of joining the over 100 mammal species that have already disappeared from earth within our lifetime. It is estimated that one quarter to one half of all known species living today could be extinct within twenty years. And this number will continue to increase if we don't actively do something about it. I didn't write this book as a scientific journal or as reference material, but as a means to put faces to a few of the animals currently at risk of extinction.

By 2020, lions and tigers in the wild may be all but extinct. That is less than ten years away. Sixteen species of life (including animal, plant, insect, bird and reptile) reportedly go extinct every day.

After I left a career in real estate, I started to become fascinated with the unique personalities of the animals that I photographed at zoos. As you'll see by the images included in this book, I was often able to make eye contact with many of the animals as I quietly stood in front of their enclosures. I observed how readily they sensed a visitors presence, and how eager some species were to 'pose' for the camera. For example, at the Audubon Zoo in New Orleans the Gorillas took as much enjoyment of the visitors as we did the Gorillas. One particular male Silverback was a real charmer, and the attendant close to his cage mentioned that he liked to ham it up anytime there was a camera pointed in his direction. While I stood observing the animals, in near proximity and without hurry, I became an advocate for all beings that share our planet. I began to study books on our endangered wildlife and watched wildlife shows and documentaries, and better understood how we are in a race to preserve the biodiversity of our planet, and that although all wildlife may be beautiful or intriguing in their own right, they are also critical components in the balance of all life.

While researching information for this book, I discovered that there is not always consensus on the numbers projected as remaining in the wild. Even with the best and most advanced technology and research, it is difficult to accurately count wild animals. When a specific animal inhabits a region where the wild areas are being taken over by growth in human population, development, farming or industrialization, it is obvious that the food supplies needed by wildlife will decline and with it the native population of a species. Global warming affects all life on earth.

There are a number of books on endangered wildlife that are much more detailed than this one. As impressive as some of these books are, I wanted to offer more of an introduction that is easily read and with photographs which portray the animals in as natural a setting as possible. I wanted to show animals that the average person, on a trip to a sanctuary or zoo in the United States, can see for themselves.

Regardless of the way the message is delivered, all agree that we have a world wide problem, and that we have to take steps now if we are to prevent future extinction of any species, including human. *In the past 200 years we have lost more species of life than in the prior 2000 years total.*

I have also learned that the preservation of 'keystone' species is of particular importance as these species are those upon whose survival so many other life forms rely for their own existence.

Many of the people that I speak with on my various trips around the country are interested in the topic of threatened animal species, but are not sure what, if anything, they can do about it. Many express a general dislike of zoos, even though they haven't been to one in years and do not know of their wider mission. Some of those with strong feelings against zoos have pets (that also once lived in the wild) and feel comfortable caging their dogs when they leave the house, and at night when they go to bed. Many more feel that the issue is just 'too big' for any one individual or group to have an impact. Although we may not be able to halt the destruction of our wildlife as solo activists, there are many reputable preservation groups, sanctuaries and associations that can accomplish small miracles with our support. This book was created to give a wider voice to all of the groups that work daily to preserve and protect our fragile wildlife.

To those who shun a 'caged' animal and who feel that they are in those cages just to be 'displayed for human enjoyment', I have to add that this is not the case, more often than not. First, fewer zoos today use the cages you might remember as a child. Many hold their animals in open environments - protecting visitors, and the animals, with moats and other natural barriers - which ecologically match the environment where the species are native. If you haven't been to one of the larger zoos in the past ten years, it may worth a visit. You, too, may become more excited about the function of zoos and their treatment of animals. Second, every large and reputable zoo has a wide range of species preservation activities that the public rarely sees or hears about. They display the animals, yes, which brings in the financial resources they need to continue with their work.

Do your best to support the many groups that are working to prevent extinction. If they do not get the financial support they need then the only place you'll see our beautiful wildlife, in the not too distant future, may be in pictures.

For those who believe that zoos capture only wild animals and then 'cage' them, it may be noteworthy that 80% of the animals in zoos are born at the zoo. Those animals are "zoo ambassadors" and are there to let visitors get closer to animals that zoos and conservation groups are preserving and protecting.

Hopefully, by seeing an animal first hand, people will be moved to give support to the organization's existence and programs.

What Leads to Extinction?

There are a number of factors that can have an impact on species survival. Most frequently mentioned as causes for the decline of various species (which includes humans):

- Competition for resources (such as habitat destruction by humans, natural catastrophe, development, logging and deforestation).

- Hunting and 'harvesting' (using rare animal meat as a food source, parts of animals being used for some alternative medicines, and trophy hunting).

- Illness/disease (some by way of use of pesticides).

- Introduction of 'alien' species (animals introduced into the wild where they are not naturally found, resulting in a competition for resources and unnatural predatory activity).

- Pollution (no need to explain to anyone who has seen the news or read a newspaper).

- Climate change (a major contributing factor for many notable species).

What Are The Categories of Risk?

There are several organizations that determine the level of risk that the various species experience in the wild: state, federal, and international (CITES and IUCN).

According to *IUCN (the International Union for Conservation of Nature)*, there are six levels of risk that are assigned to mammals which face various threats to their survival (already extinct being the seventh). This information is often referenced on identification signage that you will see at zoos.

> NT - Near Threatened
> LR/CD - Lower Risk/Conservation Dependent
> VU - Vulnerable
> EW - Extinct in the Wild
> EN - Endangered
> CR - Critically Endangered
> EX - Extinct

Critically Endangered is assigned by the IUCN when the population of a species has been reduced by 90% in the 10 years prior and that the trend is a potentially irreversible reduction in the species.

Endangered is defined as when the population has declined by 70% within the past ten years and is a potentially irreversible reduction in the species.

According to the IUCN, in 1996/1998 there were 3,314 threatened vertebrates (mammals, birds, reptiles, amphibians and fish). The number as of 2006 was 5,966. Mammals alone increased in the CR, EN and VU categories during an eight year period from 180 (in 2000) to an estimate of over 500 as of the most recent information (2008). A total of 76 mammals were noted as extinct, and 2 were extinct in the wild.

For anyone who thinks that this is an issue that does not affect the United States: according to IUCN there are 1,192 living organisms in the U.S. that are listed as Threatened, and over 1,100 that are Extinct, Extinct in the Wild, Critically Endangered, Endangered or Vulnerable. This is the Red List Category at home.

On the U.S. (federal) level, *The US Endangered Species Act*, enacted in 1973, uses the following categories in their rankings:

T = Threatened
SOC = Species of Concern
EXPN = Experimental Population, Non-Essential
E = Endangered

The state level endangered species list and categorization will vary from state to state and will concern itself with the species indigenous to that area.

CITES (the Convention on International Trade in Endangered Species of Wild Fauna and Flora) is an international agreement between governments. It's aim is to ensure that international trade in specimens of wild animals and plants does not threaten their survival. They also have classes of protection.

I = includes all species threatened with extinction which are or may be affected by trade.

II = includes all species who may become threatened unless trade in specimens of such species is subject to strict regulation in order to avoid utilization incompatible with their survival.

Why Should We Be Concerned?

Anyone who has heard of The Butterfly Effect knows the impact that each life form has on another. (If you'd like more information on this theory, you can find a good explanation at: http://en.wikipedia.org/wiki/Butterfly_effect.)

Each being's existence provides another being with sustenance, nutrition, social camaraderie and/or protection. Any time there is a significant drop in one species, any other animal that relies on them is also effected.

For example, the Yellow-billed Oxpecker consumes the tiny ticks that live on the Wildebeest. This bird's grooming helps to prevent illness in the Wildebeest. The Dung Beetle's reliance on animal feces has an impact on the pasture ecosystem, facilitating a continued deposit of nutrients needed by grasses that provide nutrients for grazing animals. In other words, they clean up and redistribute the droppings of large animals, which is why in the wild you don't see poop levels up to the elephant's ears. Even the American prairie dog, a cornerstone species that lives in the 'American Serengeti' of the United States, supports over 100 other species of life. Their habitat, which used to cover over 100 million acres, has been reduced to 2% of the land they once inhabited.

Biodiversity is defined by Wikipedia as *"the degree of variation of life forms within a given ecosystem, biome, or an entire planet. Biodiversity is a measure of the health of ecosystems. Greater biodiversity implies greater health. Biodiversity is in part a function of climate."*

A dramatic change in population can also result in an imbalance in the food chain. This can cause populations of some species to expand, while another declines, resulting in further competition for resources and a destabilization of the ecosystem.

Grazing animals also have an impact on the health of soil, both for farming and for plant life. Many grazers eat harmful fungi and keep the variety of plant life in balance. The amount of carbon dioxide increases when plant life is destroyed, and the impact on human health from climate change has already been documented. Plants and animals, insects and fish - any might hold the key to cures for human illnesses. We already use the benefits of organic foods and natural, homeopathic cures. It is estimated that 25% of the drug ingredients the pharmaceutical industry uses come from plants and animals.

As stewards of our tiny planet, we must preserve and protect all species that share this space in our universe. We would want future generations to see that we cared for our planet, and all life forms that exist here.

"All things are connected. Whatever befalls the earth, befalls the sons of the earth. Man did not weave the web of life; he is merely a strand in it. Whatever he does to the web, he does to himself." Chief Seattle

How Can You Make a Difference?

By getting to know what is causing the reduction in the population of a species, you can give appropriate support to one or more of the organizations that work to reduce that impact on the affected life form. There are a myriad of activities that you can get involved in that will help to preserve all life, including the endangered species, and help to prevent other species from moving up the endangered list.

- Learn about the living beings on the lists of currently endangered and threatened wildlife, both from a world (planet) perspective as well as within your own backyard. Most likely, you will find that there is at least one endangered animal, reptile, plant, fish, insect or bird in your area. You can download the IUCN Red list from the Internet.

- Find out what you can do at home to change history. It may be as simple as eliminating specific pesticides or planting more vegetation indigenous to your area.

- Visit your local zoo, sanctuary, wildlife animal refuge or conservation area and support their work through your donations. The true goal of zoos, conservation groups and sanctuaries, worldwide, is the protection of core areas, where animals can survive in their native habitat. 'Adopt' an animal through any one of the zoos or conservation groups. Check out World Animal Foundation for a list of available 'adoptions'.

- Volunteer at a wildlife rescue center or zoo, plant trees, recycle, develop educational materials, rescue injured wildlife, grow plants indigenous to your environment, work gratis for animal activist organizations.

- Boycott animal products: fur, animal 'trophies', ivory, coral and jewelry or clothing with those components. Let your government (local, state and federal) know that animal 'trophies' brought into the U.S. after safari hunts are unacceptable. More than five hundred animal trophies (heads, pelts, etc.) were "legally exported" into the U.S. in 2008, according to CITES.

- Be sensitive to environmental issues (a direct bearing on the habitat losses for so many of our endangered animals, including human, is the effect of global warming). Whatever you may, or may not, believe as to the extent of global warming, isn't it more prudent to act on the side of caution?

- Get behind the groups that need funding. All of them rely on individuals, corporations and governments to provide the financial resources necessary to accomplish their work. Let your elected representatives know that you believe that this is a wise use of our financial resources and that you will support legislation that will benefit all life forms on earth. Also consider leaving a legacy through a donation in your will.

- Spend some quality time searching the Internet for wildlife related information, and discover what resources are out there to help you to become an activist for all living things. Many groups will have petitions to sign, leaders and decision makers to contact, and special activities to support. There are Facebook pages for a multitude of groups that are solutions-oriented animal activists, including large and small zoos and wildlife conservation groups. These pages will provide the reader with additional activities in which to become involved, as well as information and animal images and videos to peruse.

Have Our Efforts Succeeded in The Past?

According to the Center for Biological Diversity, the Endangered Species Act, enacted by the United States in 1973, has been effective. Many of the wildlife preservation organizations, sanctuaries and zoos, that are referenced in this book have contributed to the saving of a species, and in accomplishing the following;

The Bald Eagle was once listed as endangered when, in 1963, the wild population was estimated at just over 400. Through a ban on DDT, and aggressive breeding and relocation efforts, the population as of 2006 was estimated at close to 10,000.

In Yellowstone National Park, Grizzly Bears have increased from about 200 in 1975, to over 500 in 2005.

The Manatee was listed as endangered in 1967 due to a serious decrease in the population. Through aggressive conservation efforts the population increased to 1,478 animals in 1991 and to 2,812 in 2007.

The American Alligator was once listed as threatened, primarily due to hunting. Since controls have been implemented and enforced, the Alligator has been either down-listed or taken off the threatened species list.

There were fewer than 50 Florida Panthers in the wild twenty years ago. By 2003 the population had increased to almost 100.

Both the Indian and White Rhino have been brought back through conservation efforts. Although not totally out of danger, the Indian Rhino's population has increased from under 200 at the start of the twentieth century, to over 2,500 today.

According to the Association of Zoos and Aquariums, Species Plan (SSP) programs have helped bring several endangered species back from the brink of extinction, including Black-footed Ferrets, California Condors, Bongos, African Antelopes and Red Wolves. Other programs have not, unfortunately, had the same success so far: Lowland Gorillas, Andean Condors, Giant Pandas and Snow Leopards, among others, are still under threat.

They are looking to you for help

All the photographs that follow were taken at zoos, wildlife parks and animal sanctuaries around the country.

Visit our wildlife and take some of your own photographs. If you see a specific animal that you would like to visit in person, check with your local zoo. They can tell you the best place to find a particular species.

Most importantly, assist conservation and preservation activities in any way you can.

E N D A N G E R E D

AFRICAN LION

Natural Habitat: Africa

Existing in the Wild : 20,000

Estimated Population in 1940 : 450,000

Two thousand years ago more than a million lions roamed the earth.

It is projected that they could be extinct by 2020.

E N D A N G E R E D

CHEETAH

Natural Habitat: Africa to India

Existing in the Wild : 7,000 - 10,000

Existing in the Wild one hundred years ago: 100,000

V U L N E R A B L E

JAGUAR

Natural Habitat: Arizona, California, Central and South America, Louisiana, Mexico, New Mexico, Texas

Existing in the Wild : 15,000

Listed as Endangered : 1972

The Jaguar has lost more than 37% of it's range of habitat according to the Wildlife Conservation Society.

ENDANGERED

AMUR LEOPARD

Natural Habitat: Africa, Asia, India, Korea

Existing in the Wild : 55

Listed as Endangered : 1972

Amur leopards are one of the most endangered species on the planet
and the most endangered Big Cat.

V U L N E R A B L E

AMUR TIGER

Natural Habitat: Asia, China, Korea, India, Indonesia, Malaysia

Existing in the Wild in 2010: 1,000

Existing in the Wild a century ago : 100,000+

E N D A N G E R E D

SIBERIAN TIGER

Natural Habitat: Russia, China and North Korea

Existing in the Wild : 350-400

Existing in the Wild a century ago : 100,000 +

This Siberian Tiger is one of only five tiger subspecies to have survived
out of the eight that existed in the 1940's.

VULNERABLE

FLORIDA PANTHER (COUGAR)

Natural Habitat: Southern Florida

Existing in the Wild : 80-120

Listed as endangered: 1967

Estimated Population in 1970 : Believed to be Extinct

ENDANGERED

CLOUDED LEOPARD

Natural Habitat: Southeast Asia, China

Existing in the Wild : Less than 10,000

An accurate count is difficult since the cat is solitary and difficult to track.

The population is, however, declining, due to habitat loss.

VULNERABLE

CARACAL

Natural Habitat: Africa and the Middle East

Existing in the Wild : Unknown (rarely seen in the wild)

IUCN Lists the Caracal as "Least Concerned".

CITES lists as Appendix I for Asian populations.

E N D A N G E R E D

BARBARY SERVAL

Natural Habitat: Algeria, Africa

Existing in the Wild : Unknown due to their elusive nature.

Of the 13 Subspecies listed on CITES Appendix II,

one is listed as endangered.

Servals are already extinct in the Cape Province of South Africa.

VULNERABLE

ANGOLA COLOBUS

Natural Habitat: Congo Basin, Uganda, East Africa

Existing in the Wild : Unknown, but in decline.

The Black Colobus and Ursine Colobus subspecies are listed as vulnerable.

E N D A N G E R E D

DRILL

Natural Habitat: Equatorial West Africa

Existing in the Wild : 3,000

The population has been declining in all known habitats for decades.

ENDANGERED

PYGMY CHIMPANZEE

Natural Habitat: Congo (Zaire)

Existing in the Wild : Less than 50,000

The population has declined sharply in the past 30 years.

Chimpanzees and Bonobos are our closest relatives.

ENDANGERED

WOLF'S GUENON

Natural Habitat: Western Nigeria

Existing in the Wild : Unknown

Once Considered Extinct, they are now listed as Endangered/Near Extinction

E N D A N G E R E D

BLACK HANDED SPIDER MONKEY

Natural Habitat: Bolivia, Peru, Brazil, Panama

Existing in the Wild : 2,000
There has been an 80% decline in population in the past 45 Years.
IUCN lists 1 species as Vulnerable, 4 as Endangered, and 2
as Critically Endangered.

E N D A N G E R E D

SPIDER MONKEY

Natural Habitat: Bolivia, Peru, Brazil, Panama

Existing in the Wild : 2,000

There has been an 80% decline in population in the past 45 Years.

IUCN lists 1 species as Vulnerable, 4 as Endangered, and 2

as Critically Endangered.

E N D A N G E R E D

SILVERBACK GORILLA

Natural Habitat: Congo (Zaire), Rwanda, Uganda

Existing in the Wild : 480

Estimated Population in 2000 : 700+

Protection efforts have succeeded: There has been a 26% increase in

population in one habitat (2011 Census)

ENDANGERED

GOLDEN LION TAMARIN

Natural Habitat: Brazil

Existing in the Wild : Less than 1,000

**The IUCN warns that extreme habitat fragmentation from deforestation gives
the wild population little potential for any further expansion.**

E N D A N G E R E D

WHITE CHEEKED GIBBON

Natural Habitat: China, Laos, Viet Nam

Existing in the Wild : Unknown, but declining
The IUCN reports no observation of this species
in China since 1990.

ENDANGERED

SIAMANG

Natural Habitat: Indonesia, Malaysia, Sumatra

Existing in the Wild : 23,000 (2002 Sumatra Census)

Estimated Population in 1980's : 360,000

ENDANGERED

BLACK SQUIRREL MONKEY

Natural Habitat: Central and South America

Existing in the Wild : 5,000

Population in the 1970's: 200,000

The population has continued to face habitat loss.

E N D A N G E R E D

BORNEO ORANGUTAN

Natural Habitat: Borneo and Sumatra

Existing in the Wild : 40,000 - 50,000
There has been an estimated population decline of 14%
in the past several decades.

VULNERABLE

MANDRILL

Natural Habitat: African Rain Forests

Existing in the Wild : Unknown
There has been an estimated population decline of 30%
in the past 30 years.

VULNERABLE

HOWLER MONKEY

Natural Habitat: Brazil

Existing in the Wild : Unknown
Several species of Howler Monkeys could be extinct within 35 Years.

E N D A N G E R E D

CHIMPANZEE

Natural Habitat: Africa

Existing in the Wild : 150,000 - 250,000

Estimated Population in 1900 : 1 - 2 Million

V U L N E R A B L E

BEARDED SAKI

Natural Habitat: South American Amazon

(Photo of White Faced Saki)

Existing in the Wild : Unknown
The Bearded Saki is listed by CITES as Appendix II.

T H R E A T E N E D

MANGABEY

Natural Habitat: Africa to Asia

Existing in the Wild : Unknown

*The Association of Zoos and Aquariums (AZA) has developed a Species
Survival Plan (SSP) for Mangabeys.*

ENDANGERED

BONOBO

Natural Habitat: Africa

Existing in the Wild : 30,000

Discovered in the 1970's, 98% of their genetic makeup is the same as humans.

E N D A N G E R E D

SUMATRAN ORANGUTAN

Natural Habitat: Borneo and Sumatra

Existing in the Wild : 6,600

There has been an estimated 14% decline in population

in the past several decades.

This is the only species of great apes native to Asia.

E N D A N G E R E D

WESTERN LOWLAND GORILLA

Natural Habitat: Central and West Africa

Existing in the Wild : Lowland Gorilla, 50,000; Cross River Gorilla, 300
In the 1980's the population was greater than 100,000+
Gorillas are very intelligent and have even learned human sign language.

E N D A N G E R E D

GUEREZA COLOBUS MONKEY

Natural Habitat: Africa and Asia

Existing in the Wild : 20,000-30,000
The Colobus Monkey is noted on the IUCN Red List as Data Deficient.

ENDANGERED

POLAR BEAR

Natural Habitat: Alaska, Canada, Denmark, Norway, Greenland, Russia

Existing in the Wild : 20,000-25,000

It is estimated that by 2050 there will be a two thirds decline in
population of the Polar Bear, and and they may potentially be
extinct by the end of the century.

ENDANGERED

LARS GIBBON

Natural Habitat: India to Indonesia, Sumatra, Borneo and Java

Existing in the Wild : Unknown

Estimated Population in 2000 : 300-500

Northern White Cheeked Gibbons

ENDANGERED

GIANT PANDA

Natural Habitat: Central China

Existing in the Wild : 1,000-2,000

Existing in Captivity : 100

Zoos pay the Chinese Government $1 Million a year to house Pandas.

E N D A N G E R E D

BACTRIAN CAMEL

Natural Habitat: China, Mongolia

Existing in the Wild : 600 in China, 350 in Mongolia

Estimated Population in 1980 : 600 in Mongolia

COTTON TOPPED MARMOSET

Natural Habitat: Costa Rica to Columbia

Existing in the Wild : 6,000
Deforestation has taken more than three quarters of
their original habitat.

This species is listed as one of the 25 Most Endangered Primates.

E N D A N G E R E D

RED CHEEKED GIBBON

Natural Habitat: China, Laos, Viet Nam

Existing in the Wild : Unknown but declining.
The average home range for a pair of Gibbons is 8.5 Acres
and their habitat is being destroyed at 32 acres per minute.

E N D A N G E R E D

GREVY'S ZEBRA

Natural Habitat: Kenya and Ethiopia

Existing in the Wild : 2,000 - 2,500

Estimated Population in 2000 : 15,000

Grevy's are the largest, wildest and most untamable of the zebra species.

VULNERABLE

AFRICAN ELEPHANT

Natural Habitat: Africa

Existing in the Wild : 10,000

Estimated Population in 1970: 400,000

Estimated Population Prior to 1970 : 1.3 Million

V U L N E R A B L E

MALAYAN SUN BEAR

Natural Habitat: Southeast Asia, Myanmar, Laos, Cambodia, Vietnam, Southern China, Malaysia

Existing in the Wild : Unknown

Sun Bears are sometimes domesticated as pets,
and the only predators for the Sun Bear to fear are Human.

E N D A N G E R E D

ASIAN ELEPHANT

Natural Habitat: Asia

Existing in the Wild in 2003 : 40,000-60,000
It is estimated that there has been a 50% decline in population
in the past 60 years.

E N D A N G E R E D

BROWN LEMUR

Natural Habitat: Madagascar and Mayotte

Existing in the Wild : Unknown

Threats: loss of habitat and local hunting.

E N D A N G E R E D

BLACK RHINOCEROS

Natural Habitat: Africa

Existing in the Wild : 2,700

Estimated Population in the 1980's : 350,000

Only five of the thirty original species have survived the past thirty years.

The Indian Rhinoceros is also Endangered.

T H R E A T E N E D

KOALA

Natural Habitat: Eastern and Southern Australia

Existing in the Wild : 40,000-60,000

Estimated Population in 1900 : 1 Million +

E N D A N G E R E D

RED RUFFLED LEMUR

Natural Habitat: Madagascar

Existing in the Wild : 1,000-10,000

Madagascar is considered one of the world's most important biodiversity hotspots, with lemur conservation being a high priority.

More than 200 of this species have been bred in zoos and returned to the wild.

E N D A N G E R E D

PROSERPINE ROCK WALLABY

Natural Habitat: Australia

Existing in the Wild : Unknown

Listed as Endangered in 2004 by the IUCN due to habitat destruction.

T H R E A T E N E D

RING TAILED LEMUR

Natural Habitat: Madagascar

Existing in the Wild : Unknown

This is one of the most recognizable of the endangered Lemur species.

T H R E A T E N E D

GERENUK

Natural Habitat: Djibouti, Ethiopia, Kenya, Somalia, Tanzania

Existing in the Wild : Unknown
The Gerenuk is listed as a conservation dependent species
by the IUCN (1996).

ENDANGERED

ABBOTT'S DUIKER

Natural Habitat: Tanzania

Existing in the Wild : 1,500

*Duikers are very rare in the wild, and the first photograph of the Abbott's Duiker
was taken in 2003.*

T H R E A T E N E D

THOMSON'S GAZELLE

Natural Habitat: Kenya, Tanzania

Existing in the Wild : 500,000

There has been a population decline of 60% between 1978–2005.

T H R E A T E N E D

OKAPI

Natural Habitat: Democratic Republic of Congo (Zaire)

Existing in the Wild : 10,000-20,000

In 1992 the Congo established the Okapi Wildlife Reserve.

E N D A N G E R E D

RED WOLF

Natural Habitat: Mexico, Southeastern United States

Existing in the Wild : 100-120

Red Wolves were declared Extinct in the Wild in the 1980's

There are more than 40 Species Survival Plan (SSP) facilities working with Red Wolves in the United States today.

V U L N E R A B L E

BROWN HYENA

Natural Habitat: Southern Africa

(Photo of Spotted Hyena)

Existing in the Wild : 5,000-8,000 (Brown Hyenas)

Existing in the Wild : 27,000-48,000 (Spotted Hyenas)

The Spotted Hyena's international conservation status is Lower Risk;

Conservation Dependent.

E N D A N G E R E D

GRAY WOLF

Natural Habitat: North America, Europe and Northern Asia

Existing in the Wild : 12,000 - 16,000 (North America)

Wolves do not adjust well to expanding human population.

The Gray Wolf was once the world's most widely distributed animal.

E N D A N G E R E D

NEW ENGLAND COTTONTAIL

Natural Habitat: Connecticut, Maine, Massachusetts, New Hampshire, New York, Rhode Island, Vermont

Existing in the Wild : Unknown
The Cottontail occupies less than 25% of their original habitat.

The Cottontail is a candidate for protection under the

U.S. Endangered Species Act

E N D A N G E R E D

KEY DEER

Natural Habitat: Florida Keys

Existing in the Wild : 300-800
The population of the Key Deer was near extinction in the 1950's.

E N D A N G E R E D

SOUTHERN RIVER OTTER

Natural Habitat: Argentina, Chile

Existing in the Wild : Unknown, but declining.

The species was listed as endangered in 1976.

Habitat loss and hunting are the main causes for population decline.

So, can you help us? Or are you still thinking about it?

Resources

If you want to become more familiar with a species of mammal that is currently endangered (only a minuscule number are featured in this guide), you can find an enormous amount of information everywhere on the Internet, at your local library and in bookstores. Become more aware, more knowledgeable of the crisis that confronts all of us.

In this section are listed a number of organizations and associations that work to save one particular species, and many more that have committed their resources to save larger, even mixed, populations of species.

If you want to see more photographs of animals that are of special interest to you, the internet has websites where photographers, activists and vacationers post images that they've taken in the wild, on safari, at conservation areas and zoos. Check out www.Flickr.com. In the search area, enter the species in which you have an interest. Google Image and Yahoo Search are also good sources for photographs and information.

Visit your local zoo or wildlife park. Not all are created equal, and some are not as progressive as others in the way they display their animals. *Availability of operational funding is not equal and not all zoos receive all of the funding required to provide superior environments.* However, all animal caretakers are committed to the protection, preservation, and humane care of the animals in their charge. They don't want to be the last refuge for animals at risk of extinction. But without the commitment of zoos and wildlife sanctuaries, we would be in greater danger of a faster decline or decimation of many species. Some of the work that has been performed by zoos and conservation areas include animal husbandry, treatment of injury and illness, habitat protection, activism for the benefit of all living creatures, and educational programs for all ages and levels of education. All zoos play a role in maintaining genetic and bio-diversity.

To learn more about what zoos accomplish, you can research more about the part they play in the preservation of threatened, and non-threatened species. The Association of Zoos and Aquarium's (AZA's) Species Survival Plan (SSP) manages the breeding programs for a number of species that benefit through a healthier existence and perpetuation of their species. Many of the conservation groups who also 'display' birds and animals, focus on returning wildlife to their native habitat. One example is the Center for Birds of Prey in Maitland, Florida. Since their existence, they have treated over ten thousand sick or injured raptors (including eagles and owls) and returned most of them to the wild. Big Cat Rescue, in Tampa, Florida has treated, and released back into the wild, a large population of native species, including bobcats, panthers and ocelots.

Take time to visit the National Geographic website. It contains more information than you can ever absorb in a quick review. The photographs are stunning and will mesmerize you. They also have an entire section on the environment and animal conservation.

There are a number of great television channels for watching animal adventures and documentaries. *NatGeoWild* (*Crimes Against Nature, Expedition Wild*, and specials such as *Mystery Gorillas* - to name just a few), *Animal Planet* (which aired the award winning *Life* series), and the *Smithsonian Channel*. You can become an activist and a couch potato at the same time.

Below are listed several of the major contributors to the efforts to preserve and protect our endangered, vulnerable and at-risk wildlife. All will benefit from donations, and you will benefit by visiting their website to become more familiar with the issues today. By joining their Facebook pages you will be getting involved.

WORLD WILDLIFE FUND - This international activist organization promotes the protection of all endangered wildlife. Founded in 1947, WWF employs over 150 personnel and has over a half million members. Their Mission Statement: *"Defenders' mission is to protect species and the habitats upon which they depend. In doing so, we focus on preserving the health of our nation's rich biological heritage..."* In addition, *"...WWF safeguards hundreds of species around the world, (as well as) focus special attention on what we consider "umbrella species," since helping them helps numerous other species that live in the same habitats."* On their website you can make a donation, and find information on many of the species they are working diligently to protect. You can get information on hosting a local event for wildlife, thereby getting more information out to the general public. (http://www.worldwildlife.org/)

WILDLIFE CONSERVATION SOCIETY - WCS was founded in 1895, and according to their website, *"During our 115 years, we have forged the power of our* global conservation work and the management of our five parks in New York City to create the world's most comprehensive conservation organization. With a commitment to protect 25 percent of the world's biodiversity, we address four of the biggest issues facing wildlife and wild places: climate change; natural resource exploitation; the connection between wildlife health and human health; and the sustainable development of human livelihoods. While taking on these issues, we manage more than 200 million acres of protected lands around the world, with more than 200 scientists on staff." (http://www.wcs.org/)

THE NATURE CONSERVANCY -Their statement, *"You depend on nature-we're here to save it. We're working with you to make a positive impact around the world in 32 countries, all 50 United States and your backyard."*

The Nature Conservancy was founded in 1951 and have more than one million members. Also listed on their website are ways to support the cause. (http://www.nature.org/aboutus/visionmission/index.htm)

NATIONAL WILDLIFE FEDERATION - Founded 75 years ago, NWF is the nation's largest conservation organization. Their mission statement is to *"inspire Americans to protect wildlife for our children's future"*. They have a number of fun conservation programs directed at children. (http://www.nwf.org/)

NATURAL RESOURCES DEFENSE COUNCIL - The NRDC mission is *"to safeguard the Earth; it's people, its plants and animals and the natural system on which all life depends."* Issues addressed on their website are: Curb Global Warming, Save Endangered Wildlife and Wild Places, Create the Clean Energy Future, Revive the World's Oceans, Stem the Tide of Toxic Chemicals, and Accelerate the Greening of China. *"NRDC was founded in 1970 by a group of law students and attorneys at the forefront of the environmental movement."* (http://www.nrdc.org/)

INTERNATIONAL FUND FOR ANIMAL WELFARE: Founded four decades ago, this group has over 1.2 million supporters. Their mission statement is *"to create a better world for animals"*. They are best known for their activism in protecting the Harp Seal, but they are also vocal regarding our domestic animals and wildlife in other countries. (http://www.ifaw.org/ifaw_united_states/)

ALLIANCE FOR GLOBAL CONSERVATION: On their website you can get information regarding a bi-partisan bill, The Global Conservation Act of 2010. Through their link you can contact your elected officials to let them know that you support the United States government's efforts to address the international conservation crisis. (http://www.actforconservation.org/)

The USFWWS (United States Fish and Wildlife Service) website will give you additional information on their Endangered Species program activities. Their Facebook page highlights the different species that are at risk of extinction in this country. http://www.fws.gov/

The AZA, (Association of Zoos and Aquariums), was founded in 1924. On their website, *"Over the last five years, AZA-accredited institutions supported more than 3,700 conservation projects with $90,000,000 annually in more than 100 countries. In addition, zoo and aquarium scientists contribute to hundreds of conservation, biology, and veterinary science publications."*: http://www.aza.org/.

Our zoos accomplish so much more than 'animal display'.

Conservation - Zoos are involved in a broad range of research, including climate disruption and ocean conservation. They work on 'reintroduction programs' (returning ill or injured animals to the wild after treatment), and take in young animals, orphaned in the wild, unable to care for themselves.

Education - All age groups learn about the native and non-native species found at zoos. Zoos give school children exposure to a field with career potential. I've often observed the children as they watch the animals and wonder which ones will grow up to be a zoologist, conservationist, veterinarian or scientist. Any one of those professionals could be the one to make a discovery that would save a species, including human. At one of the zoos I visited, a young girl about ten years old came up to me after watching the cheetahs for about ten minutes. She was studying my camera, and asked if I was a 'picturologist'. I smiled and showed her my camera, but didn't correct her terminology. Maybe she will take that fascination with cheetahs and cameras and develop a successful career in the field of nature photography, or help save the cheetah from extinction.

Animal Care and Management - Animals in the wild have benefitted from infectious disease treatments that were developed at zoos. More than 200 members of the AZA were involved in the rescue and rehabilitation of wildlife after the Deepwater Horizon oil spill. And when most people have moved on to another news event, the AZA is still there at work, more than a year later.

Sanctuaries

The following is a small sampling of U.S.-based groups that provide shelter for wildlife with the goal of returning them to the wild, if possible, or giving them a natural environment to live out their remaining lives:

BIG CAT RESCUE: Located in Tampa, Florida, Big Cat Rescue was founded in 1992, and operates on a 45 acre site. BCR treats and returns to the wild (or rehabilitates and provides long term care for those who cannot be returned to the wild) lions, tigers, Caracals, Panthers, Bobcats and leopards, among others. (http://bigcatrescue.org)

THE ELEPHANT SANCTUARY IN TENNESSEE: Founded in 1995, they state that it is the nation's largest natural habitat refuge developed for African and Asian Elephants. They operate on over 2700 acres and give sanctuary to more than 24 elephants. (http://elephants.com/)

BORN FREE USA PRIMATE SANCTUARY is located in San Antonio, Texas. According to their website, *"The Primate Sanctuary is a division of Born Free USA. Our mission is to provide nonhuman primates as high a quality of life as we can, with as little human interference as possible. The 186 acre Sanctuary, located near San Antonio, Texas, is currently home to more than 500 individuals, many of whom were rescued from abusive or exploitative situations."* At this location, more than 500 Macaques, Baboons and Vervets are able to live range-free. (http://www.bornfreeusa.org)

WILDLIFE RESCUE AND REHABILITATION: Founded in 1977, WRR is located on a 187-acre facility near San Antonio. Each year, over 5,000 animals are brought to the facility. The majority are rehabilitated and released back into the wild. (http://wildlife-rescue.org)

With a little Internet research you can find a wildlife sanctuary near you to visit and to support.

Selected Bibliography & Sources

Wikipedia, the Free Encyclopedia. Web. 11 Mar. 2011.
<http://en.wikipedia.org/>.

UNEP-WCMC. 24 May, 2011. UNEP-WCMC Species Database: CITES-Listed Species
http://www.unep-wcmc-apps.org/isdb/CITES/Taxonomy/index.cfm/isdb/CITES/Taxonomy/index.cfm

Welcome to CITES. Secretariat of CITES. Web. 12 Mar. 2011.
<http://www.cites.org/eng/resources/species.html>

Center for Biological Diversity. Web. 5 May 2011.
<http://www.biologicaldiversity.org>.

Endangered Species - EndangeredSpecie.com. Web. 6 Apr. 2011.
<http://www.endangeredspecie.com/>.

U.S. Fish and Wildlife Service Home. Web. 2 May 2011. <http://www.fws.gov/>.

Rockwell, Dr. Mark. Endangered Species Coalition. Web. 6 May 2011.
<http://www.stopextinction.org/>.

"Programs and Policy - Defenders of Wildlife." Defenders of Wildlife - Protection of Endangered Species, Imperiled Species, Habitats. Web. 6 Apr. 2011.
<http://www.defenders.org/programs_and_policy/>.

UCN Red List of Threatened Species. Version 2010.4. <www.iucnredlist.org>.
Downloaded on 15 March 2011.

UCN Red List of Threatened Species. Version 2010.4. <www.iucnredlist.org>.
Downloaded on 7 April 2011.

http://www.earthsendangered.com/search-groups2_sM.html>. Downloaded on 11 March 2011.

Additional Organizations You May Want to Research

- Endangered Species Coalition

- stopextinction.org

- forevertigers.com

- aboutmyplanet.com

- National Wildlife Federation

- Association of Zoos and Aquariums (AZA)

- National Geographic

- African Wildlife Foundation

- Great Apes Survival Partnership

- Endangered Species International

- Save China Tigers

- Earthtrust

- Alliance for Global Conservation

This is far from an all inclusive list, but it's a place to start.

There is still time to make a difference.

Already Extinct

Don't look for us as we're among the mammals who've become extinct since the 1930's.

- Japanese Wolf (1930's)

- Desert Rat Kangaroo (1935)

- Desert Bandicoot (1943)

- Japanese Sea Lion (1950's)

- Bali Tiger (1940's)

- Mexican Grizzly Bear (1960's)

- Caspian Tiger (1950's)

- Javan Tiger (1976)

- Syrian Wild Ass (1928)

- Bubal Hartebeest (1923)

About the Author

I left full time employment in early 2010 after working forty years behind a desk. When I stopped working, I needed a creative outlet and I was mystified as to what to do with the unrelenting adrenaline rushes I couldn't leave behind at the office.

Sometimes the best way forward is by going backward.

I loved photography before I switched gears to parenthood and a career. My daughter suggested that I take the camera back out, permanently, and that I give it the same intensity of focus (pun intended) as I did my career. About that time a friend had suggested that I visit the local zoo. "What? Me? I don't like zoos! I haven't been to one since I was a child". Little did I know how they had changed, and that zoos today have a larger mission statement than I had ever realized. I've now photographed animals in zoos from San Diego to the Bahamas. And during these trips I bonded with another species each time.

Friendly suggestions from two friends started me on a new journey.

I've learned more about issues greater than a day-to-day job. I've learned about the environment, the treatment of animals, and the ever-present risk of some species extinction. In my former life I always wanted to make a difference. In this reincarnation of my spirit, I am determined to continue that philosophy.

Go and watch the animals watching *you*. Learn about *their* life and death challenges. See what others are doing to keep them in existence. If you haven't been to a big city zoo in ten years, you may be pleasantly surprised!

Disclaimer

The study of mammals in the wild is a difficult task and the population data may change from researcher to researcher and from year to year. In addition, the habitats are changing daily as animals are forced to move to survive. What has been included as data in this text has come from reliable sources and resources as of 2011.

This book is not intended to be scientific or to be relied upon for any research purposes. It's sole purpose is to inspire the reader to support the groups that are working to protect earth's wildlife and to help others become aware of the most familiar animals facing extinction today.

All of the photographs that are included in this book were taken by the author.

ENDANGERED

Still waiting for your help...

Made in the USA
Charleston, SC
21 October 2011